C000143735

THE POLICE
SELF-DEFENCE
HANDBOOK

BRIAN EUSTACE

A & C BLACK · LONDON

First published 1990 by
A & C Black (Publishers) Ltd
35 Bedford Row, London WC1R 4JH

© 1990 Brian Eustace

ISBN 0 7136 3265 8

All rights reserved. No part of this
publication may be reproduced, stored
in a retrieval system, or transmitted in
any form or by any means, electronic,
mechanical, photocopying, recording
or otherwise, without the prior
permission in writing of A & C Black
(Publishers) Ltd.

A CIP catalogue record for this book is
available from the British Library

Typeset by August Filmsetting,
Haydock, St Helens
Printed and bound in Great Britain by
Whitstable Litho Ltd, Whitstable, Kent

ACKNOWLEDGEMENTS

I gratefully acknowledge the contribution made to this book by the
following:

David Mitchell for helping to produce the text, and

Mark Moores and **Kate Wheatley** for demonstrating the techniques.

B. Eustace
Stratford upon Avon

CONTENTS

FOREWORD

Police officers fulfil many roles and a great deal of work goes into training them to cope with the demands of those roles. Their sphere of knowledge must include such things as community and race relations, social skills of policing, law and its procedure, and public order. However, one of their main functions is 'to apprehend offenders against the peace'. Officers are taught how to determine the occasions and circumstances when it is necessary and lawfully correct to arrest offenders. Regular updating and amendment brought about by changes in legislation are systematically incorporated in their training.

In most cases, the arrest of offenders is carried out with co-operation and without violence. However, there are occasions when police officers are confronted with violence. This means they must respond with force in order to prevent disorder and to arrest offenders. Until 1973, the methods employed to achieve this were based upon unarmed combat techniques used in the armed forces.

The Police Service subsequently reviewed a wide variety of self-defence methods and martial arts. The review did not provide an obvious and immediate solution to its self-defence needs in the form of any one of these disciplines; rather, it appeared likely that a combination of judo and aikido techniques would prove most appropriate.

Through the efforts and expertise of a then-serving police officer, Brian Eustace, a special form of self-defence was devised. It was recognised both in Britain and in Japan, where it is known as **Taiho jutsu** ('techniques of arrest'). Its techniques emphasize the avoidance of injury and the safety of officers when making arrests. They have been updated through experience and now form the basis of probationer training. In this book, the author gives a detailed description of the range of techniques, together with their variations, which are the basis of Taiho jutsu.

The skills needed to operate the techniques have to be acquired and regularly practised if they are to be used effectively in the wide variety of circumstances which confront police officers in their daily duty.

INTRODUCTION

Owing to an escalation of violence in recent years, an increasing number of people from all age groups have become interested in learning how to defend themselves from attack. The most popular forms of self-defence taught in Britain have been imported from Japan, Korea and China. The majority of these forms provide good exercise and are absorbing hobbies. However, because of their strong, traditional background, they often take a long time to learn. Indeed, it may be months or even years before a student reaches a reasonable standard for the purposes of self-defence.

In the normal course of events, the vast majority of the population will not come face to face with physical violence. Their only experience of it will be through staged fights in films. Unfortunately, many self-defence courses appear to be structured on the staged versions rather than on reality. In fact, the attacks are tailored to fit favoured self-defence techniques. Furthermore, to conform to the martial art image, if often appears that these techniques are more violent than the initial assault. Yet it is the task of the genuine instructor to educate students to control rather than to escalate the level of violence. Sadly, this strategy is unpopular, primarily because it isn't spectacular. Nevertheless, this is the correct method of self-defence, if only because over-reaction may well result in the defender being prosecuted.

Taiho jutsu's primary objective is twofold: to teach the police officer how to respond effectively to an attack and to make safe an attack in order to avoid serious injury. The techniques of control are of secondary value only and use the principles of joint leverage to restrain without causing undue injury. Surprisingly, it would appear that choice of techniques is not as important as the manner in which they are taught and practised.

The techniques have been set out in seven sections to make them easier to learn. The first four sections comprise basic techniques and attacks. Then there is a section dealing with the techniques of groundwork. The last two sections consist of free fighting/sport techniques intended to build fast responses. The various forms of free play progress from a one-against-one format to a two-against-one format, leading finally to competition.

This system is not in any way superior to other forms of self-defence; it is just that at the present time it is the one best suited to the requirements of the Police Service.

Note Throughout the text individuals are referred to as 'he'. This should, of course, be taken to mean 'he or she' where appropriate.

SELF-DEFENCE AND THE LAW

Before beginning the course, it will be as well to confirm how self-defence relates to the law. Section 3 of the Criminal Law Act of 1967 states that authority is given for the usage of reasonable force in self-defence situations. The questions to be determined when assessing the use of force under this section are:

was the force used necessary, or reasonably believed to be so?
was the force proportionate to the wrong which it sought to avoid?

You must ask yourself whether a physical self-defence response is necessary at all. In some situations, the only violence which actually comes about is of the verbal kind. Insults, however, are not sufficient grounds for using self-defence techniques. A physical response may be justified only when there is a real likelihood of attack and then it must be appropriate to the nature of the threat which you believe you face. Obviously if the aggressor is armed, or is substantially larger than you are, then you will have commensurately good grounds for using force.

In other words, you must determine how serious the potential threat to you actually is. Of course, in the fraught circumstances immediately before a potential attack, you could not be expected to make as prudent an assessment as hindsight might dictate. However, it is best always to err on the side of caution and consider your own well-being first.

> **How serious is the threat made against you?** The law allows you only to make such a response as is necessary to nullify the danger that you are facing. You must take no action which would escalate the level of violence.

The serving police officer does not have the facility of simply withdrawing from a potentially violent situation and therefore the self-defence techniques which follow have been designed so that he can effect an arrest with the minimum of force appropriate to the task. Self-defence techniques – such as spearhand thrusts into the eyes – are effective, yet are disqualified except in cases of mortal danger. This category of techniques has been omitted from the police course and replaced with grappling techniques which use controlled leverage.

Members of the public are not obliged to engage with an attacker and must, wherever possible, try to withdraw – even if this means giving over money or property.

Where there is a serious threat to life or limb, then you may be justified in taking up and using a weapon. However, you must never take up a weapon which you are not prepared or are unable to use skilfully, in case it is turned against you. The police course describes ways of using the truncheon, but in all cases hard blows to vulnerable areas of the head and body are avoided.

TACTICAL THINKING

Awareness

The best form of self-defence relies upon good observation and intelligent assessment to recognise and, where possible, avoid potential hazard. Awareness is a state of mind – of knowing what is happening, or may happen. It comes about when all available and relevant facts are gathered and interpreted correctly. The trick, therefore, is to be as aware as possible without becoming paranoid!

When the possibility of danger is detected, it becomes difficult not to concentrate on it to the exclusion of everything else. Perhaps the would-be attacker is struggling in a restraint hold, and concentration is devoted to keeping him immobile. This narrowing of awareness can mean that the arrival of his friends goes unnoticed until it is too late. The lesson is clear: maintain a level of general awareness at all times.

Verbal communication

Use effective communication to reduce the hazard level. Speak distinctly, so there is no possibility of being misunderstood. Whilst the other person is listening to you, he is incapable of thinking clearly about the next move. Choose words carefully and put yourself in the position of the listener. This may help you to select an approach which leads to complete understanding.

Your manner of speech may be authoritative, or what is called 'facilitative'. The authoritative approach tries to direct the behaviour of the attacker by means of an authoritative command, order or, slightly less authoritatively, through a suggestion or proposal. There is also an informative approach which imparts knowledge; you might tell the other person, 'If you keep shouting and swearing like that, you'll cause a breach of the peace – and get yourself into trouble!' Confrontational behaviour seeks to raise the other person's consciousness by drawing attention to his behaviour in a helpful way. You could say something like, 'I understand why you feel the way you do – but don't you realise that you aren't helping yourself by being so aggressive?'

Prescriptive approaches try to get the other person to vent his emotions safely. The sort of thing said might be, 'You're obviously very angry indeed – can't we talk about it and try to sort things out?' Another approach tries to get the other person to solve the problem for himself. You might say, 'Try to see this situation from another person's point of view.' A supportive approach commiserates with the other person; you understand why he feels the way he does.

Body communication

However, not all communication uses words and it is widely believed that 75% of information which we receive comes to us in non-verbal forms. Facial expression can indicate what the other persons is feeling. For example, anger is generally expressed through a scowl and narrowed eyes. If the face is red and the voice is loud, then blood is still being pumped through the skin capillaries and has not been shunted to the muscles in preparation for an imminent fight or flight response. Compare this with the pale face and quiet voice of the person who is about to attack you.

Body attitude also provides clues. Standing erect with chest out and fists clenched indicates power, confidence and assertiveness. The distance apart that two people stand is also relevant. Each person has his own 'personal space' and feels threatened when another intrudes into it. The aggressive person will move into your personal space and then perhaps aggravate matters further by poking you with a finger. A pointing finger is generally taken to be a symbolic club and can therefore be interpreted as another sign of aggression.

Assessing the situation

However, it is dangerous to come to any firm conclusions on the basis of non-verbal communication alone. Check out what the person is trying to say and consider everything together before arriving at an assessment.

Despite all reasonable observation, evaluation and communication, an element of risk will always remain. When this risk presents itself, it is better to avoid a physical response if this is at all possible. Be prepared to swallow insults and offer apologies, even when they are unwarranted. Such actions are those of a strong person acting from a position of strength. However, when all other ways have failed and a response is inevitable, then you must make a total commitment to it if there is to be any chance of success at all.

Follow a tactical procedure when evaluating a potentially dangerous situation. Take into consideration:

1 the seriousness of the crime committed
2 the size, age and weight of the offender
3 the apparent physical ability of the offender
4 the number of persons present who are also involved, or who might become involved

5 weapons possessed by or available to the offender
6 whether the offender is known to have a history of violence
7 the presence of innocent persons or potential victims in the area
8 whether the offender can be recaptured at a later time
9 whether evidence is likely to be destroyed.

Some of these points might appear irrelevant to a member of the public who is considering using self-defence, but a closer examination will reveal a definite relevance. Taking the first item, the police officer would respond differently to youths stealing apples than he might to youths badly beating a member of the public. This item relates to the degree of response dictated by the seriousness of the physical threat posed. Refer to the previous chapter for more information.

The second and third items also help to grade the level of physical response called for. Knowing something of the attacker's previous history (item six) helps to grade your response.

The fourth item is important because what begins as a one-to-one confrontation may well turn into something entirely different if the attacker's associates take exception to what you are doing to their friend. Item seven is of consequence because it may prove necessary to intervene in order to save a less able person from injury. Intervention made without an initial tactical appraisal, however, could result in both you and the first victim being injured. If there is any likelihood of this happening, then it is better to summon help as speedily as possible.

The following factors must also be considered:

– your own size, physical ability and defensive skill
– the number of helpers on hand
– your immediate reaction in case of sudden attack
– any weapons or means of restraint available to you
– legal requirements.

The larger and stronger you are, the greater the choice of action available to you. However, even large and skilled individuals should avoid over-confidence. This causes you to under-estimate the attacker because you are taking into consideration only his weaknesses. It is one of the surest routes to being injured, or even killed. If this were not enough in itself, over-confidence can also lead to other members of the public being exposed to unnecessary risk. An intelligent and alert person is one who is always aware of the attacker's potential strong points and is prepared to deal with them. The alert person can cope with the unexpected, whereas the over-confident person cannot. Therefore, over-confidence must be suppressed – both for your own protection and safety, as well as that of the public.

In the face of overwhelming odds, the best immediate self-defence response is to run away as quickly as possible!

Think about the situation before you decide what action to take. How serious is the threat made against you? How big is the opponent? Is he armed? Are his friends lurking around? How well are you able to defend yourself? What will you do when he attacks?

PREPARING TO TRAIN

Fitness

The techniques used in this course are not strenuous in themselves, but the process of learning them may show up a lack of fitness. Skill acquisition requires that a technique be repeated several times over, but if the student isn't fit enough to do so, the rate of learning will be slowed. Moreover, the learning process works best when the student is not mentally or physically tired. It therefore follows that you must have sufficient fitness to cope with the training session. Exactly how much is 'sufficient' will vary according to your starting level of fitness, the intensity and duration of the training session and the number of sessions in a unit period of time.

The purpose of self-defence training is not to make you fit and time spent in doing that is essentially time wasted. Come to training already fit enough to benefit from it. The types of fitness required are stamina, strength, speed and suppleness.

Are you fit enough to get the maximum benefit from your training? Skill is best learned when you are not gasping for breath or about to collapse from exhaustion. Make sure you are fit enough to train before you enrol on a course.

Stamina

Begin by building the right kind of stamina. This is achieved by working the heart muscle moderately hard for around 20 minutes each day. Use running, cycling, swimming, or exercise aids, such as rowing machines, to build your aerobic fitness platform. Work at a rate which will allow you just to be able to finish the full twenty minutes. After a week or so of this training, you will be able to work through the full lesson without suffering unduly from fatigue. Having said that, you may find muscles aching that you didn't know you had. If this is the case and stiffness develops after training, then expect it to go away during the first few minutes of the next session.

Strength

Strength training gives the techniques a greater lee-way for application. Very weak people are obliged to develop a high degree of skill in order to make their techniques work. Stronger individuals can get away with less skill and more techniques will work for them. Any self-defence system which claims that strength is unnecessary for effectiveness is not being truthful. There is no doubt that when the level of skill remains constant, the stronger you are, the more chance of success you will have.

Strength exercises work on particular muscle groups and it is important to recognise those which need strengthening and those which are already strong enough. Although multigyms and free weights are very good for strength-building, there is no reason why the body's own weight can't be used.

Speed

Speed is also an important aspect of self-defence training. Heredity determines which type of muscle fibres preponderate in your body and this imposes an ultimate limit. Where speed becomes a limiting factor, it remains possible to increase strength and, by doing this, maximum power can be extended. For our purposes, power is the product of the strength of a muscular contraction and the speed at which that contraction occurs.

Suppleness

Suppleness refers to the range of movement at a joint, or at a series of joints. If the joint is able to move smoothly through a full range of movement, then the potential for realising maximum power is increased. There is also a benefit in safety because if you are supple, then going for that last centimetre or so of reach will not pull a muscle.

Stamina refers to your ability to train hard over a long period. Speed means how fast your whole body or any individual limb can move. Strength is the ability of your muscles to contract against a loading. Suppleness is the range of movement at a joint. Power is the ability of muscles to move strongly and at speed.

Exercises

There now follows a series of exercises designed to improve the aspects of fitness so far discussed.

Running on the spot

Running on the spot can be a simple exercise for improving stamina (if it is done at a low intensity for long enough), a means of developing localised muscular endurance in the legs and a form of speed training. This second aspect is brought out by running harder over shorter periods. The legs quickly tire, but become more used to functioning in the presence of increasing levels of metabolic waste products. Rest by interposing periods of less intense running between bouts of high-intensity work. If you prefer, you can substitute skipping for running.

Speed training consists of moving the whole body or its limbs as quickly as possible over a very short period. Use running on the spot, but raise your knees high and pump your arms vigorously. Allow a rest and repeat the exercise several times.

Squats

Squats can also be used to improve stamina in the leg muscles and, with certain modifications, they can be used to increase strength. The addition of

Fig. 1 Squats can be used to develop endurance and power. Sink down until your knees are bent no more than 90 degrees, then straighten them with an appropriate degree of force.

Fig. 2 Build explosive power by thrusting hard from the squat position so that both of your feet clear the ground.

an explosive jumping action changes the exercise into a power-developer. Stand with your feet a shoulder-width apart and sink your body until the knees bend through ninety degrees (fig. 1). Do not exceed this degree of flexion – especially if you have poor knee joints. Pause, then thrust your legs straight once more. Work at an easy rhythm over a long period to develop a general, low-intensity endurance. Increase the rate over a shorter period to extend your endurance and interpose breaks of lower-level activity between sets of repetitions.

Build strength by carrying a weight across your shoulders (but keep your back straight at all times!). Build explosive power in the legs by thrusting clear of the ground as you straighten up (fig. 2).

Burpees

Burpees are a whole-body endurance exercise that should be performed for at least ten repetitions. Begin from an erect stance, then drop to your knees, fingertips brushing the mat (fig. 3). Thrust your legs out behind you, keeping

Fig. 3   Burpees begin from an erect stance. You should then drop until your fingers brush the floor.

Below **Fig. 4**   Thrust both legs out, balancing yourself on your hands and the balls of your feet.

Fig. 5 Spring back into the crouched position, then thrust yourself clear of the ground.

Fig. 6 Jump high, separating your arms and legs as much as possible to form a star shape. Retrieve them in time for landing.

your body straight and take the weight on your fingertips and the balls of your feet (fig.4). Spring back up with the feet into the 'gathered' position and thrust up into a vertical jump (fig.5).

'Star jumps'

'Star jumps' work the leg muscles in a series of jumps which take the whole body clear of the floor. Splay your arms and legs as wide as possible (fig.6).

Press-ups

Press-ups can be used in many ways. The first way is as an upper body strengthening exercise. Straighten your elbows and support your body on fingertips (or flats of hands) and the balls of your feet. Don't sag in the middle, or lift your hips too high. Lower your body by flexing your elbows, until your chin just brushes the mat (fig. 7). Hold this position for a second or two and then thrust powerfully back to an arms-locked position once more. Work at a steady pace and aim to complete at least ten. Some people may find that their upper body muscles are so weak they can't manage even one press-up. If so, simply drop your knees to the mat (fig. 8). Increase work-load by resting your feet on something, for example, a chair (fig. 9).

Fig. 7   To perform a press-up, lower your body until your chin brushes the floor – but keep your back absolutely straight.

Fig. 8   Persons with weak upper body muscles can perform press-ups by first lowering their knees to the mat. This reduces loadings on the shoulders.

Fig. 9   Increase the training effect of press-ups by resting your feet on a chair.

Fig. 10   Develop power by thrusting up so strongly that your hands clear the mat.

Use press-ups also as a local endurance exercise by aiming to do as many repetitions as possible. You might perform ten, have a ten-second break, then do eight more followed by another break, six, four, two and a final one. Increase work-load further by seeing how many press-ups you can do in, say, thirty seconds. Develop power by thrusting up so hard that your palms clear the mat (fig. 10).

Lower your body forwards and down between your arms (fig. 11). Let it skim over the surface of the mat as your elbows lock straight and your back arches (fig. 12). Then reverse the action until you return to the opening press-up position.

Fig. 11 Your body swoops down and forwards between your hands.

Fig. 12 Arch your back, dropping your hips to the mat whilst straightening your elbows fully.

Sit-ups

Sit-ups work the abdominal muscles in various ways. Lie on your back, keeping at least a slight bend in your knees. Failure to do this can increase the possibility of back injury. Bring your hands to the sides of your head – but don't tug on your neck – and look down at your knees. Pull your body clear of the floor and rise to a vertical position, hold, then return slowly back. You may find that your feet jerk clear of the mat. If so, then hook your feet under something or have a partner press them down (fig. 13). Vary the training effect by changing the angle of your bent knees. Bringing your heels close to your backside will engage a different group of muscles to a different extent than when the knees are virtually straight.

Twist your body to each side as you sit up (fig. 14), increasing work-rate to improve stamina. Allow breaks between successive work intervals. Strengthen your stomach muscles by sitting up from an inclined surface.

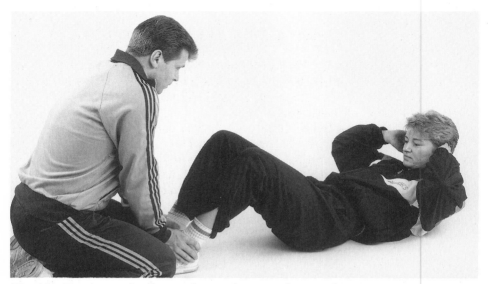

Fig. 13   For sit-ups, hook your feet under something, or have your partner press down on them. This prevents your legs, instead of your shoulders, from rising.

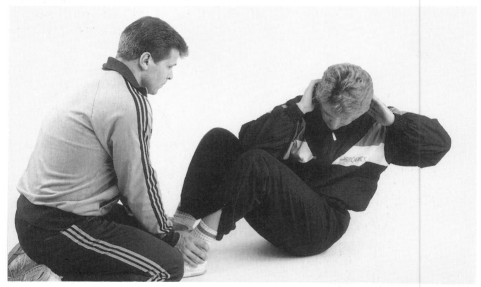

Fig. 14   Alter the training effect of sit-ups by twisting your body to each side alternately as you sit up.

Stretching exercises

Warm muscles are less viscous and can be stretched more easily and with greater safety than cold ones. Therefore, save the suppleness exercises until

later in the programme. Take the joint to be stretched to the limit of movement and hold it there for at least ten seconds before allowing it to return to
a less stressed position. Never stretch to the point of actual pain since this is
counter-productive.

Work the ankles through their full range of movement by crossing one leg
over the other and taking the joint in your hands. Next, kneel with your
back straight and the feet fully extended under your thighs. Maintain this
position for at least 30 seconds.

The knee joint is already flexible and needs no work doing on it. The
hamstring muscles on the back of the legs can be usefully stretched by
bending forward at the waist and touching the mat with the fingertips. More
supple students may find it possible to place the palms against the mat.
Whichever is used, the knees must be kept absolutely straight. As a variation on this theme, stand on your palms and then try to straighten fully your
knees (fig.15). Alternatively, reach through between your legs (fig.16) and
then straighten up, arching your back in the reverse direction.

You can also perform hamstring stretching exercises by sitting with the
backs of your legs pressed firmly to the mat. Combine lower back and hamstring stretches by rolling back onto your shoulders. Splay your hands to
maintain balance and drop your feet to the mat (fig.17). Return to a sitting
position, with your legs opened wide. Lean between them with hands out-
stretched and sweep from side to side (fig.18). Return to a standing position,
open your feet wide and lower your weight over one leg as you straighten the

Fig. 15 Stretch your hamstrings by
standing on the palms of your hands
and then straighten your knees.

Fig. 16 Increase hamstring stretch by
leaning between open legs, extending
your fingertips as far as possible.

Fig. 17 An interesting way to stretch your hamstrings uses gravity. Roll onto your shoulders and let the weight of your legs pull them down – but keep your knees straight!

Fig. 18 Lean forwards as far as you can and sweep your body from side to side.

other (fig. 19). Keep both feet flat to the mat as you sink your weight down as far as possible. Then move across onto the other leg.

Lean your body from side to side in smooth sweeps and increase the training effect by linking your hands back to back above your head (fig. 20). Twist your body from side to side (fig. 21) and finally take it through a full circle, with arms trailing (fig. 22). Reverse the direction of sweep on each repetition.

Take your wrist in your other hand and work it through its full range of movement. Press the palms of your hands together and move the forearms downwards (fig. 23). Then point the fingers away from you and repeat the exercise. Finally put the backs of your hands together and lift your forearms.

Twist your head smoothly from side to side. Then lower it until your chin

Fig. 19 Lower your weight onto one foot, straightening the other leg. Lean forwards to keep your balance.

Left **Fig. 20** Increase the stretch on your lateral muscles by thrusting your straight arms above your head.

Centre **Fig. 21** Twist your body smoothly from side to side.

Right **Fig. 22** Move your trunk in wide circles, turning first in one direction and then the opposite way.

Fig. 23   Press the palms of your hands together and move them downwards.

brushes your chest. Throw your head back as far as it will go. Lower your head sideways onto each shoulder in turn and conclude by rolling your head down across your chest, over your shoulders and back as far as it will go. Change direction with each repetition.

   This is by no means an exclusive list of exercises; you can select those which are appropriate to your needs and ability. It is better to train a little every day, or every other day, than to work intensively and then not to train for a long period. Prepare youself for training by limbering up with a few exercises of your choice. These should aim to raise the temperature of the working muscles, leaving you with a healthy glow. Loosen the muscles and joints which you will be working during the session.

   A 'cool-down' is equally important after the session and ten minutes spent working at a gradually slowing tempo of exercises will result in less stiffness during the following day.

Choose those exercises which are necessary to improve your fitness in areas where it is lacking. Add these to an aerobic fitness base that allows you to work through the whole training session without undue fatigue.

FALLING CORRECTLY

Many self-defence situations lead to one or both opponents falling, whether as a result of being tripped, thrown, or simply through loss of balance. The object of this initial part of the training, therefore, is to teach you how to fall safely. Begin by training on a cushioned surface, using a technique progression that initially sets up the body correctly and then goes on through a series of steps of increasing difficulty.

The front breakfall begins from a kneeling position, with the body upright. Lower your body and slide forwards, with elbows bent and hands turned palm-downwards in front of your face. The fingertips of both hands should be almost touching. Turn your head to the side, to avoid banging your face on the mat. Repeat this exercise a number of times until you feel confident, then try it from a half-squat and, finally, from a standing position. At no time should you reach for the mat with straight arms, since this may result in broken bones.

Rear breakfall is similarly practised through a technique progression. Step back a short distance with your right foot and lower your body so weight is above the right heel. Then roll back, whilst bringing your arms across your chest, curving your spine and tucking your chin down onto your chest. By this means, the energy of landing is converted smoothly into a rolling motion. Bear in mind that most real-life falls are onto a hard surface and it would be dangerous to attempt the more advanced judo-type breakfalls. The latter are designed for sport training and competition – not for self-defence.

POSTURE, DISTANCE AND TIMING

Posture refers to the way in which the body and limbs are used in a self-defence situation. One should never think of posture as a static thing – it is adopted in response to a situation and even as that situation changes, so must the posture. The object of the posture is to provide a small target, whilst leaving the body balanced and all of your body weapons immediately available for use.

Passive posture

Two postures are used in the Police Self-Defence System. The first is known as 'passive posture'. It is characterised by standing at a slight angle to the left of the opponent, with feet no more than a shoulder-width apart. Bring your hands across your body and clasp them in front of the groin. Turn your head to look at the opponent, but at the same time be aware of what is happening in the periphery of your vision.

The reason why you stand a little to the left of the opponent is that it will then be necessary for him to turn slightly in order to reach you, and this will give you more time in which to respond. Obviously you cannot step too much to the side, otherwise the opponent will simply turn his body to face you once more. Your body is angled so as to close off large areas of it – particularly the groin – from direct attack. The hand position is inoffensive, yet provides body cover.

Active posture

The second is known as 'active posture'. Take this up when you are being threatened with imminent violence. Step diagonally forwards and outwards a half-pace with the left foot and bend the knees slightly to pre-load the leg muscles with energy. The diagonal movement gives the posture lateral stability – but it must not be over-emphasised. Do not face the opponent square-on; withdraw the right hip and shoulder slightly, so you don't present a large target. Open both hands and bring them into the centre-line of your body, the left leading the right. This is an effective posture and, by not using clenched fists, it does not escalate the tension in a potential encounter.

Balance is safest when the body's weight is distributed equally over both feet. However, when the leading and trailing heels of active posture are in line, then the stance will lack lateral stability and a slight shove will be sufficient to unbalance you. Since the front foot leads the rear, the stance has good balance in the fore and aft direction and it is through this axis that most energy can be safely transmitted.

Don't stand rooted to the spot! Learn to move quickly and with balance in any direction. You must maintain a distance which causes the opponent to step forwards in order to reach you. Move as he moves; don't wait to see what he is going to do.

Movement

All movements between postures must be as quick as possible, since standing on one leg is neither the most stable nor the safest position to be in.

By moving the feet in sequence, it is possible to move quickly to the side, diagonally forwards/backwards and to advance/retreat. A swift movement in the right direction is important, because it keeps the opponent at a suitable distance. Try always to remain just out of reach and maintain your position slightly to the left of the opponent, since this keeps him at a disadvantage.

Timing

The timing of your movements and responses is also important. Move too early and the opponent will change direction as well. Move too late and his technique will reach you. Early warning of an attack is vital, but there is no way of distinguishing between a feint-type move and a committed attack. Therefore, the rule of thumb must always be to make safe, rather than to stay in there and try to cope.

Some people advise you to look at the opponent's eyes, since they narrow momentarily before a committed attack. It may be true, but lighting conditions may preclude this. Others tell you to look at the triangle formed by the opponent's head and shoulders, responding when this moves. If you have set up the correct distance, then the opponent will have to step, or at least lean well forward, to reach you. This should provide a long enough interval in which to move.

A boxer, or experienced martial artist, can throw punches without excessively following through with the body. This means that several techniques can be launched in quick succession. Less experienced attackers frequently swing widely and, when their technique misses, they take a longer time to recover posture. If you time your self-defence response as the technique is just beginning, it will not have developed its full force and your pre-emptive advance will throw the opponent into confusion. Though this sounds good in theory, in practice it requires a skilled person, capable of reacting without hesitation in the face of violence. Inexperienced individuals should make safe by withdrawing themselves from the attack and responding as the opponent is recovering his posture.

This, too, requires skill but it is less fraught with danger. In order to be successful, your withdrawal must be just sufficient for the attack to miss. Withdraw too far and it will take you as long to close distance as it will for the opponent to recover his posture.

Remember: move at the right speed, in the right direction, at the right time and above all – make safe!

THE BASIC TECHNIQUES

For ease of learning, the basic techniques are set down in four sections, each comprising four techniques. The restraint techniques are quite complex and, because of this, they are introduced early in the syllabus. They form the basis of the Police Self-Defence System and are repeated in the ensuing sections. Sections two and three teach defence against grappling and striking techniques; the fourth section shows how to use the truncheon.

In all, sixteen techniques are shown, but you need only learn eight – two from each section – for basic training. Select the techniques which you find the easiest to perform. All techniques are shown from the right side, but in the later stages of training you must also be able to apply at least one technique from the first three sections on the left.

Section one: restraint techniques

The techniques contained in this section should be applied before the opponent actively resists. The rule of thumb here is to restrain aggression before it begins. Where possible, approach the opponent from the side or rear. Approaching head-on is more dangerous, though you must still practise it because, in reality, this may be the only avenue open to you. The restraint techniques require you to be close to the opponent, so beware head butts or kicks.

> **Restraint techniques must be applied before the opponent actively resists.**
> Those selected allow you to control the amount of leverage applied, so injury is avoided. Apply the restraint technique at the first inkling of trouble.

Front gooseneck

Grasp the opponent's right wrist with your right hand. Take his elbow in a thumb-upwards grip (fig.24). Stand in left posture, close to the opponent's right side, so you neither lean forwards nor over-extend your arms. This is a

Fig. 24 Front gooseneck. Take the opponent's elbow and wrist in a firm grip. Apply the grip from behind and to the right side.

Fig. 25 Thrust the opponent's elbow forwards, whilst drawing back and lifting his forearm.

Fig. 26 Bend the opponent's wrist forwards, applying pressure to the back of it. Trap the right elbow against your chest.

Fig. 27 Reinforce pressure on the opponent's wrist by using both of your hands.

passive grip and, by talking to keep the situation under control, this may be all the force required to lead the opponent away.

If the opponent resists, apply pressure through your right hand to raise and draw back his wrist, bracing his elbow with your left (fig.25). Keep the opponent's hand pointing downwards and turn it slightly outwards. Slide your left hand under the opponent's armpit and push his forearm forwards and up. Use your right hand to apply pressure to the back of his hand, flexing the wrist (fig.26). Quickly slide your left hand through and under the opponent's arm, joining with your right hand. The opponent's limb is trapped in the crook of your left elbow and is held there by downward pressure on the wrist applied by both of your hands (fig.27).

Remain close to the opponent so you can control him effectively. At the first hint of reaction against the hold, press down harder on the opponent's flexed wrist. If necessary, increase leverage by sliding your grip towards his knuckles.

Thumb lock

A variation of the above technique applies pressure to the thumb rather than to the wrist. This has the advantage of requiring less force to gain control, though it may prove difficult to take and keep hold of the thumb.

Begin from the passive hold described above (fig.28). Draw back your right

Fig. 28 Thumb lock. Begin from the passive hold position.

Fig. 29 Push the opponent's elbow forwards and draw back the wrist, so that his upper body tilts forwards.

Fig. 30   Slide your left hand down and seize the opponent's thumb.

Fig. 31   Bring the opponent's wrist forwards, controlling it with both hands.

Fig. 32   Wedge the opponent's right elbow against your side.

hand and push forwards with the left, so the opponent's right arm is brought back and up (fig.29). Quickly slide your left hand down and seize the opponent's thumb (fig.30). Push his wrist forwards, controlling the opponent with both hands (fig.31). Do not slacken your hold on the thumb. Wedge the opponent's right elbow against your side, bracing the hold with your right hand (fig.32). Apply pressure to the opponent's thumb at the first sign of resistance.

Do not be over-enthusiastic in applying leverage, since this hold is painful and can cause panic reactions with some opponents.

Rear gooseneck

This technique also applies control through leverage against the opponent's thumb. Begin from the passive hold position and slide your left hand quickly down the opponent's arm, seizing hold of the thumb (fig.33). Take the captured arm up the opponent's back, bracing it there with your right forearm (fig.34). Control is applied through pressure applied to the thumb (see rear view, fig.35).

Left **Fig. 33**   Rear gooseneck. Seize the opponent's thumb with your left hand. *Centre* **Fig. 34**   Take the opponent's hand up his back and brace it there.

Right **Fig. 35**   Control the opponent by holding tightly to the trapped thumb, preventing him from moving away by means of the shoulder brace.

Entangled arm lock

The hands are reversed from the passive hold position, so your right hand grasps the opponent's elbow and the back of your left hand pushes back

Fig. 36 Entangled arm lock. Take the opponent's elbow in an over-arm grasp whilst pushing his wrist back with your left hand.

Fig. 37 Lever under his forearm and over his upper arm, steadying him with your hand against the front of his shoulder.

Fig. 38 Bring the opponent back and onto his tip toes by applying pressure to the front of his shoulder.

against his right wrist (fig.36). Push his elbow down whilst sliding your left arm upwards and across the front of the opponent's arm. Take your hand over the back of his shoulder. Prevent him from moving away by placing your right hand on the front of the attacked shoulder (fig.37). Use this brace to bring the opponent back and onto his toes (fig.38). Move the opponent forwards to break his balance and apply leverage across his bent elbow.

Section two

This section teaches responses to situations in which you have been held. The principle of distance is no longer available to you, so use timing to ensure that your response is swift and appropriate. The object is to regain quickly the initiative.

The four techniques of this section are split into two pairs. The first pair shows how to respond to the early stages of a grapple, before the opponent has been able to secure a grip. The second shows what to do once the grip has been secured.

Side arm lock

The side arm lock is used to respond to a head-on attack. The opponent steps forwards and attempts to grab your shirt-front (fig.39). Take his arm, even as it is reaching for you, seizing the wrist in both of your hands (fig.40).

Fig. 39 Side arm lock. Maintain a correct distance so the opponent must step forwards to grab your shirt front.

Fig. 40 Take his wrist in both hands.

Keep the hand pressed firmly to your chest as you swivel your hips, running your left elbow over the top of his straightened arm (fig.41). Step out with your right leg, drawing the aggressor off balance (fig.42) and bend both

Fig. 41 Press the trapped hand firmly to your chest as you turn away. Your left forearm overlies the opponent's elbow.

Fig. 42 Lean away, drawing the opponent forwards and off-balance whilst over-extending the attacked arm.

Fig. 43 Bring the wrist up and press down with your left elbow, so the opponent is levered down to the mat.

knees. Keep the opponent's little finger uppermost as you apply pressure to the wrist and elbow, bringing the opponent face-downwards to the floor (fig.43).

Take your left hand away and bend the opponent's arm across it, applying the necessary pressure through your right hand (fig.44). Grasp the opponent's upper arm with your left, levering against his shoulder in the manner of an entangled arm lock. Brace his right shoulder with your right arm (fig.45). Look up once the lock has been properly applied to check that your opponent's friends aren't in the vicinity.

Side arm lock applies leverage across the opponent's straightened arm. Hold the trapped wrist firmly and wedge the arm tightly against the side of your body. Apply downward pressure with your left elbow as you draw the arm out.

Once the opponent has grabbed you, it is no longer possible to use distance to your advantage. Use timing instead, making sure you act before he has secured his hold.

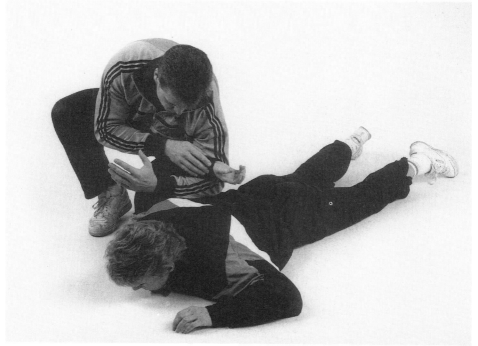

Fig. 44 Bend the opponent's right arm with the crook of your elbow. Steady his wrist with your right hand.

Fig. 45 Apply an arm entangle as you brace the attacked shoulder with your right hand.

Wrist turn

This response is also applied on the move. The attacker steps forwards and attempts to grab your shirt-front. Turn to the side, even as the push is landing, and take his right wrist with your left hand, so the thumb presses

Fig. 46 Wrist turn. Take the opponent's wrist with an over-hand grasp of your left hand. Your extended thumb should cross the back of his hand.

Fig. 47 Twist your body away, drawing the opponent forwards and off balance.

into his knuckles (see from other side – fig.46). Use the combination of grip with turning action to draw the opponent's arm straight, whilst taking him off balance (fig.47). Twist your hips around until you face the opponent square-on. Your left foot slides back as this happens. Reinforce your grip on his wrist with your right hand, so your thumbs cross (fig.48).

As you turn forwards, the opponent's elbow will bend. Press with your

Fig. 48 Reinforce the grip with your right hand, crossing both thumbs on the back of his wrist. Step around strongly with your left leg.

Fig. 49 A combination of the turning motion and bending the opponent's fingers towards his shoulder drives him down and onto his back in front of you.

Fig. 50 Keep the opponent's arm straight as you step around his head.

Fig. 51 Pull him onto his face.

Fig. 52 Flex his elbow and change the grip into a reverse gooseneck hold.

Right **Fig. 53** Bring him to his feet but keep his forearm under control at all times.

thumbs against the back of his hand, combining this with the last stages of the body-turning action. This combination applies considerable leverage across the wrist joint and drops the opponent onto his back (fig.49). Maintain the grip, so he can't roll away from you. Step quickly around his head, drawing his arm out straight. Keep the wrist bent in a gooseneck (fig.50). Continue stepping around and pull the aggressor onto his face (fig.51).

Quickly flex his elbow and transfer your left hand into a reverse gooseneck hold applied to the right wrist. This is similar to the hold used above except that the attacked forearm is rotated and the fingers point over his shoulder. Brace his forearm with your right hand (fig.52). Then stand up, pinioning the right elbow against your left side (fig.53).

Side head lock

This is a common attack, the opponent throwing his right arm across the back of your neck and pinioning your head between his bent elbow and ribs (fig.54). Strike the opponent's groin with your right hand, using several hard blows if necessary (fig.55). At the very least, this will cause a loosening of the head lock and will allow you to act in either of two ways.

The first assumes that you can thrust your left arm up, barring it across the opponent's chin. Bring your left knee behind the opponent's right thigh and, using pressure applied through your left arm, roll the opponent over backwards (fig.56). The second method assumes that you have not been able

Fig. 54 Side head lock. This is a common form of attack.

Fig. 55 Strike the opponent's groin with one or more hard punches.

Fig. 56 Bar your hand across the opponent's face and roll him over your left thigh.

Fig. 57 If you can't force your arm up the front, then encircle the opponent's waist, grab the inside of his thigh and lift him.

Fig. 58 The rear neck lock is extremely dangerous because it cuts off the supply of oxygenated blood to the brain, causing rapid unconsciousness.

Fig. 59 Move your hips to the side and strike the opponent in the groin. Use several blows if necessary.

to drive your left arm up. Force it around the opponent's back instead and grasp hold of the underside of his right thigh with your right hand. Straighten your knees and lift the opponent (fig.57).

It is not necessary to bar across the opponent's face with your left arm. You can do equally well by grabbing his hair or collar. The object is simply to force the opponent's head back.

Rear neck lock

This is an extremely dangerous attack which, unless it is quickly countered, can lead to strangulation. The opponent attacks from behind, swinging the right forearm across your windpipe and locking the hold with the left hand (fig.58). Don't hesitate for an instant – strike back into his groin with your left fist (fig.59). Be prepared to strike several times if the first is unsuccessful, moving your hips to the side to allow a clear path for the blows. At the very least this will cause him momentarily to loosen the grip, allowing you to reach up and seize his forearm with your left hand, and his upper arm with your right.

Step forwards and bend your knees, so the attacker is drawn forwards and off balance (fig.60). Drop your right knee down to the mat as you simultaneously draw him diagonally forwards and over your shoulder (fig.61). Twist your upper body as you apply leverage.

Fig. 60 Step forwards and bend your knee so the opponent is dragged off balance.

Fig. 61 Drop your right knee down to the mat and twist your body to the left, whilst pulling down on his arm.

Unless you become very skilled at applying this technique, it is likely that the throw will not be clean and both of you will roll onto the floor. If this is so, later training in groundwork will allow you to apply an appropriate restraint hold. In a real life situation you would not attempt the throw until your groin strike had achieved at least partial success.

Section three

This section builds upon what we have already covered and teaches how to respond to the opponent's punches. The first objective is to make safe, that is, to remove yourself from danger. It is done by maintaining the correct distance, so the opponent's punch always falls short. Be prepared to move by the minimum necessary amount to ensure that this is so. Timing is also critical, since the opponent will not leave his spent punching arm extended for you to attack. You must therefore aim to catch his arm and grip it securely if what follows is to work. This will require considerable practice. Even if you fail to take the arm, you will at least have made safe.

Note that strikes are used to divert the opponent's attention. Please bear in mind that these should be used only when necessary and then with sufficient force to achieve that end – do not escalate the violence being used! Police officers especially must be able to justify their usage of strikes.

> **Always make safe in the face of the opponent's punch.** Take yourself back out of range and use the x-block to sweep a wide area clear of attacking techniques. Take hold of the captured arm and apply a suitable follow-up technique.

Kick/push down

The kick/push down defence is made in response to a committed punch to the face. If you have correctly used the principle of distance, then the opponent will have to reach forwards in order to land the punch. As the punch approaches, bring both of your forearms diagonally up and across your face in an x-block, trapping the incoming fist (fig.62). Since the block does not require a great amount of power, there is no need to make a major commitment of your arm and upper body muscles. If you do, then the block will be jerky and slow to retrieve for the follow-up. At worst, the x-block is a failsafe; at best it is a deflecting block that catches the opponent's punch high on his arm, knocking the fist upwards.

Your arms separate outwards, the right slipping over the left and taking the spent punch out and down with it (fig.63). Pull the opponent forwards and off balance. Then bring your right foot up in a snapping low kick (fig.64). Excessive force is not required, since the object is simply to divert

Fig. 62   Kick/push down. Catch the opponent's punch in the 'x' formed by your forearms. Don't use too much power as you block.

Fig. 63   Your arms separate, taking the opponent's down to your right.

Fig. 64 Snap kick to the opponent's stomach, landing with your instep and shin. Bring your foot back afterwards.

Fig. 65 Chop down on the opponent's extended arm, so the elbow is over-extended.

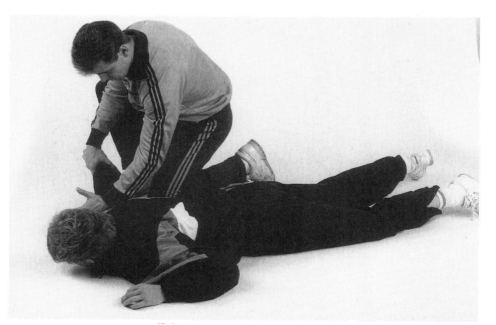

Fig. 66 Sufficient pressure on the trapped elbow drops the opponent on his face.

attention from what follows. The kick lands with the shin and instep, so turn your toes downwards and extend the foot. Power for the kick comes in the first instance from the acceleration imparted by the upper leg muscles, and in the second instance from a snapping action as the lower leg flies out. The action is something like cracking a whip.

The kick doubles the opponent up and provides time for you to retrieve your foot. Provided you have not released your grip on the opponent's right wrist, you can then continue the sequence by striking downwards with a chopping action, onto his upper arm (fig. 65). This jams the elbow joint on full extension, and by levering up on the wrist as you saw downwards with your hand-edge the opponent is brought face-down to the floor (fig. 66). Keep the trapped arm fully extended, otherwise the push down, as it is called, will not work effectively.

Knee/rear pull down

This sequence uses the same attack and x-block response. Take the opponent's arm to your right and pull it forwards (fig. 67). This time you are standing closer to the opponent and a kick would be inappropriate, so use your knee instead (fig. 68). Attack the opponent's solar plexus or ribs, then

Fig. 67 Knee/rear pull down. Take the opponent's punch down to the right, pulling him forwards and off balance.

Fig. 68 Since you are rather close to the opponent, your knee is more suitable than a kick for striking.

Fig. 69 Step around behind the opponent and put both hands on his shoulders. Draw him backwards.

step around quickly behind him – before he has a chance to recover from your knee-strike. Place both hands on his shoulders and draw him backwards and off-balance (fig.69).

Always be prepared to change your follow-up should the opponent not respond to your diversion as expected.

Left hand/arm turn

Reply to the opponent's punch with an x-block, taking his arm out to your right (fig.70). Use a back-hand slap to the opponent's face to divert his attention (fig.71), but be sure to retain your grip on the wrist. Bring the wrist up by bending the elbow and turn the fingers towards the face in a reverse gooseneck wrist hold. Thrust your left hand behind his forearm and jam your hand edge against your own wrist (fig.72). Then straighten your left elbow, applying leverage to the gooseneck and forcing the opponent to bend backwards and lose balance (fig.73).

Keep hold of the wrist as you follow the attacker to the mat, extricating your left hand and using it to reinforce your grip on the opponent's wrist. Kneel on the side of the aggressor's neck – but do not apply too much pressure! Your other knee jams against his ribs (see fig. 74 and, for a view from the front, fig. 75). Apply leverage to the gooseneck by drawing back with both arms.

Fig. 70   Left hand/arm turn. Take the opponent's punch to the right.

Fig. 71   Bring your left hand up in a back-handed slap to the opponent's face.

Above **Fig. 72**   Fold the opponent's arm back and force your left forearm past the crook in the elbow.

Right **Fig. 73**   Straighten your left elbow, forcing him backwards and off balance.

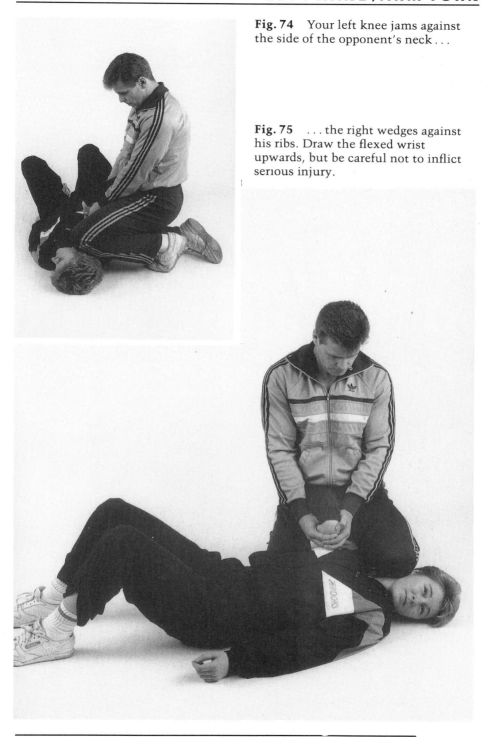

Fig. 74 Your left knee jams against the side of the opponent's neck . . .

Fig. 75 . . . the right wedges against his ribs. Draw the flexed wrist upwards, but be careful not to inflict serious injury.

Right hand/leg trip

Respond to the opponent's punch with an x-block, taking his arm to your left and gripping his wrist. Smack him smartly on the point of the jaw, using the pad of flesh at the heel of your open hand (fig.76). It is important that you drive the head back, otherwise he will be able to resist your follow-up technique. Bring your right arm around the side of his neck and grasp his collar, drawing his left arm across your body. Bring your right foot up and hook back with it into his lower leg (fig.77). Throw him diagonally backwards and across the front of you.

The throwing action is accomplished by thrusting your head forwards, using your hips as the pivot for this action.

Above **Fig. 76** Right hand leg trip. Use the pad of flesh at the heel of your hand to strike the opponent on the point of his jaw. Take his right arm out to your left.

Right **Fig. 77** Lean well forwards as you hook back into the opponent's leg. Twist your hips and push him diagonally backwards.

Section four

Section four of the Police Self-Defence System teaches how to use the truncheon. Members of the public may use any suitable weapon of opportunity that comes to hand; a wooden rolling pin is a good example. The truncheon must have sufficient mass to inflict bruising, yet not be so heavy that you cannot use it in a versatile way. Begin by holding the truncheon in front of the groin, using a double over-hand grasp (fig.78).

Fig. 78 Hold the truncheon in front of your groin, using a double over-hand grasp.

Truncheons make good self-defence weapons provided they are heavy enough to deal a sharp blow, yet light enough to be moved quickly and with control. The baton should not be so long that it gets caught up in clothing or furnishings.

Chest strike

The first truncheon technique teaches how to respond to a front kick by thrusting the truncheon into the opponent's shin (fig. 79). Keep your back straight and do not lean forwards, otherwise your face becomes a tempting target for a follow-up punch.

Where you apply the truncheon is also important. Blocking low on the opponent's shin is not a good idea if you don't have strong wrists. This is because the lower shin and instep have the most kinetic energy, so the baton is easily jarred loose and wrists can be sprained. On the other hand, block above the knee and the opponent's foot may well carry on through to kick you in the groin. The correct position is therefore just below the knee joint.

To mimimise the jarring impact yet further, use a positive blocking action; that is to say, thrust the truncheon into the attacking shin. Time your block so the kick is still developing. Don't wait until the attacking leg is nearly straight.

Your block will hurt the opponent's shin, and cause him to drop his foot down. Therefore, unless you act immediately, he will resume his attack with a series of punches. As soon as your truncheon strikes the shin, pull it back and thrust it strongly into the opponent's chest (fig. 80). The earlier you do this, the more effective the strike will be.

Fig. 79 Chest strike. Keep your back straight as you thrust the truncheon into the path of the kick. Be prepared for a severe impact.

Fig. 80 Don't wait for the opponent to regain composure; slam the truncheon hard into his chest, knocking him backwards and off balance.

Leg strike

This sequence uses a similar opening response to a kick (fig. 81), after which you step diagonally outwards with your right leg. Strike the opponent's left knee a sharp blow and thrust your straight left arm into his shoulder (fig. 82).

Fig. 81 Leg strike. Bar the opponent's kick with your truncheon.

Fig. 82 Rap the opponent's leg with the truncheon as you strike him in the shoulder with your left hand.

Fig. 83 Lift the opponent's leg with your truncheon and push him off balance with your left arm.

Fig. 84 The truncheon hooks under the opponent's knee.

Hook the truncheon under his knee and step strongly forwards with your left leg, thrusting the opponent backwards and off balance (fig.83). Lift the truncheon at the same time to help unbalance him (fig.84 shows the view from the other side).

The success of this technique depends upon a fast, strong advance to the side of the opponent. But do not step wide or you will be unable to control him properly.

Arm strike

The opponent steps forwards to make a committed punch to your face. Step back, if necessary, and knock the punching arm upwards with the truncheon (fig.85). Since you are blocking close to the wrist, the amount of leverage applied will be substantial, so an overly powerful action is not required. Your left hand releases the truncheon but remains in contact with the opponent's punching arm. The right swings down and strikes the opponent a sharp blow on the arm (fig.86).

Step forwards a half pace and thrust the truncheon under the opponent's left arm. Reach over with the right to jam the truncheon under the armpit (fig.87). Continue stepping around until your right side is against the opponent's left. Trap the opponent's left arm between the truncheon and your right upper arm (fig.88).

Fig. 85 Arm strike. Take a full step back and deflect the opponent's punch upwards.

Fig. 86 Rap the opponent sharply on his right arm, but maintain your left in the deflection position.

Fig. 87 Reach over with your right arm and jam the truncheon under the opponent's armpit.

Fig.88 Trap the opponent's upper arm between the truncheon and your upper arm.

Like most of the techniques used in the Police Self-Defence System, this response requires you to act on the move. Do not stand rooted to the floor! Move fluidly as the opponent moves and do not fumble or hesitate at any point, because if you do the opponent will regain the initiative.

Knife defence

A sharp knife is a potentially lethal weapon, even when it has a blade length of less than 6.5 cm (2½ in). If it is at all possible, avoid making a physical response to a knife wielder – other than running away!

However, that option may not be available to you, in which case some sort of defence may have to be made. Distance and timimg assume a new level of importance and these must be employed to keep you just out of reach of the blade at all times. The opponent must be forced into reaching out for you if you are to operate the suggested technique.

If you are carrying a coat, wrap it over your arm to act as protection, or swing it into the opponent's face. Some coaches advise slipping a shoe off and using this to protect the leading guard hand. Whether this works will depend upon such factors as whether you can slip the shoe off quickly – without falling over – and whether the shoe itself is substantial enough to withstand slashes.

In the example chosen, the opponent lunges forwards and you respond immediately by turning your hips and striking the extended forearm

Fig. 89 Knife defence. Bring the truncheon down sharply on the opponent's extended wrist.

Fig. 90 Kick the opponent in the groin, impacting with your shin and instep.

(fig.89). Immediately kick the opponent in the groin, using an extended foot position and striking with the shin (fig.90). Watch that knife at all times! Step forwards and to the inside of the knife, locking the truncheon across the back of his elbow and jamming the arm on full extension with your left elbow (fig.91). Apply leverage to the elbow, forcing his head further down (fig.92).

Step smartly around with your back leg, bending the opponent's elbow and holding him in a form of entangled arm lock (fig.93). Make certain that you bring him in close to your hip, so he can't pull his arm free. Bend your knees sharply and take him down to the mat (fig.94).

Knife defence training must be carried out with a safe blade. Aikido rubber knives are ideal for the purpose, but if these are inaccessible plastic strips may be used instead. Avoid wooden knives, because they can cause injury. The sport aikido section described in the next chapter provides a great deal of useful practice in the type of movements suitable for knife defence.

Above **Fig. 91**
Jam the opponent's arm on full extension, between the truncheon and your forearm.

Above, right
Fig. 92 Apply leverage to the elbow joint, forcing the opponent's head down.

Fig. 93 Step around with your back leg, bringing your left thigh against the opponent. Hold him securely in an arm entangle.

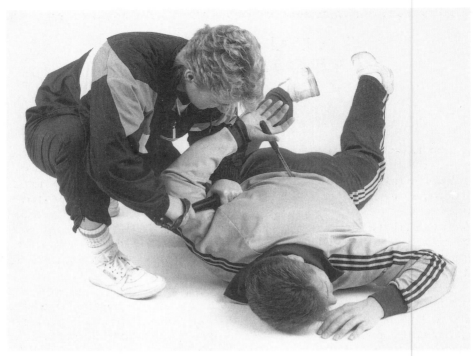

Fig. 94   Bend your knees sharply and drive him to the mat.

GROUNDWORK TECHNIQUES

A great many people misunderstand the purpose of this section of the syllabus. It is a strategy for learning how to take the initiative when both parties fall to the floor during a self-defence situation. This is not a collection of techniques intended for practical self-defence in the street, but a method of practice governed by safety rules. The rationale behind this section is based on the fact that children seem able to tumble about the floor, wrestling quite effectively as they roll over and over. Adults lose the ability to think on the ground, so the groundwork section of this syllabus aims to re-familiarise people with what it is like.

Each pair of practitioners must have enough space in which to work and the floor surface must be such as to allow relatively painless tumbling about. A judo mat is ideal for the purpose but, failing that, any large area of agility matting will suffice. It is important to wear suitable clothes and the models in this book have chosen to wear judo tunics. These are loose fitting and have no ends or buckles to cause injury. They are also quite strong and are easily laundered.

Some of the techniques involve joint locks, so it is important that good co-operation exists between partners. Release the hold the instant your partner taps you or the mat.

Scarf hold

Kneel down on your right knee while throwing your right arm around the opponent's neck. Support your body at this stage on your left foot and right hand. Then push your right foot forwards, lying across the opponent with your right side pressing against his. Spread your legs widely in order to gain stability in the face of determined opposition. Grab his right sleeve mid-way along its length with your left hand and draw his arm across your chest, tucking his wrist under your armpit. Drive your right arm under the opponent's shoulders and grab his tunic sleeve close to your left grip (fig.95).

Turn your face to your left and bring your head down low. Prevent the opponent from sitting up by pressing down with your left foot whilst applying full bodyweight against his chest. The opponent may gather his feet in and bring his left arm over your back, with the object of suddenly thrusting his hips up and causing you to overbalance forwards. Counter this by pressing down with your right foot whilst leaning back slightly. A strong opponent may try to grab your belt on the left side and, with a powerful

Fig. 95 Scarf hold. Your right hand drives under the opponent's collar and takes his right sleeve. Your left hand grips his elbow. Spread your legs wide apart and do not lean too heavily on him.

twisting motion of the hips, roll you over his chest to his left. This is why you must never rest all your weight on the opponent's chest. Even the strongest person will have difficulty in rolling you when the greater part of your weight is away from the axis of rotation. He might try to withdraw his right arm by twisting to his right and tugging hard. Respond by pressing your left elbow against your body and gripping his arm tightly behind the elbow. If necessary, lower your head and bring your right thigh under the opponent's elbow as a wedge, to prevent him from turning to the right. Secure the hold and let your opponent try various methods of escaping.

Upper hold

Sometimes the opponent is thrown or falls on his back in front of you, with his head nearest and his legs pointing away. Thrust your body forwards, so your chest slides over his. Twist in such a way that your shoulder presses down on his breast bone and reach for his belt with your right hand, slipping your arm under his. Then twist your body the other way as you reach down for the other side of his belt with your left hand. Either splay your legs widely to improve stability (fig.96), or drag up your left knee and wedge it under his left arm. The inside edge of your foot presses against the mat and the toes turn to the left.

Fig. 96 Upper hold. Your arms are thrust under the opponent, holding securely onto his belt. Turn your head to the side and lower the full weight of your upper body over his face, causing him to turn it to the side.

It is also possible to draw up both legs so that your heels touch your buttocks. In this case, the feet overlap so, for example, the instep of your right foot fits against the sole of your left. Your body must be close to the ground. Press your head down against the opponent's chest and squash his face with your chest. This will force him to turn his head sideways in order to breathe.

Hold tightly with both hands and spread your elbow on the side to which the opponent tries to roll you. Tuck your head in, so the opponent can neither slip his right hand under your chin, nor catch your head with his knees. The combination of foot positions allows you to adjust for any side-to-side movements. This hold down is effective as long as your bodies are both in the same axis.

Straight arm lock

The opponent lies on his back and you stand over him, taking hold of his right sleeve at a point above the elbow. Put your right toes under his ribs and near to his armpit. Then bend your right knee, taking full body weight over this foot. Take his right wrist in your right hand and swing your left leg in a circular motion around his head and across his throat. Lean forwards whilst bending the right knee and then sit down so your buttocks touch against

Fig. 97   Straight arm lock. Pull his arm out straight and lean back to apply leverage. Your left leg holds the opponent's head down and the right wedges against his ribs.

your right heel. Press down on the opponent's throat with your left leg and both pull and twist his arm so that the crook in the elbow points upwards. Draw it in between your legs and close your thighs on it (fig. 97). Apply controlled pressure to the elbow joint by pulling the trapped arm down to the right, levering it across your upper right thigh.

Sometimes the opponent may be holding your lapel with his right hand as he falls. It is still possible to use this technique and progress as though his hand was free. However, you will not be able to pull the arm down to the right. Instead, apply leverage by closing your thighs on the arm and then lifting your hips from the ground.

Bent arm lock

The opponent lies on his back and you kneel with your right knee close to his ribs. Watch out for his left hand reaching for your throat. Grab it in your left hand and, throwing your weight forwards, push it down to the mat. Slide your right hand under his upper arm and take your own left wrist in an over-hand grasp. Press his chest down with yours and lever his left elbow up (fig. 98). Exercise care when applying force, otherwise you may cause joint injuries. Stretch your right leg backwards if you need to increase pressure against his chest whilst improving your balance.

Fig. 98 Bent arm lock. Apply leverage by raising your right elbow from the mat – but avoid using too much force. Pinion the opponent with bodyweight, but be prepared to respond should he try to roll you off.

The self-defence application of groundwork

Always look at what limbs you have free and what targets they can be applied to. Thus in the first scenario, the attacker has rolled on top and is applying a stranglehold. Both of his hands are now out of commission whilst both of yours are free. What targets are available for them?

Obviously you can attack his groin with one or more blows. Alternatively, you could bring your right knee up, forcing him to straighten his arms, and then flick your fingertips across his eyes (fig.99). Any sudden movement towards the eyes will always cause a reflex blink, with the head turning away. If your fingers graze the cornea of his eye, they will produce copious tears and interrupt clear vision.

However, what you must not do is to jab your stiffened fingers into his eyes!

Once you have loosened his grip, you can thrust down with your left foot while levering him away with your right knee (fig.100).

Provided you can make a hard hand weapon, many parts of the opponent's body become available for attack. For example, close your fist and press the ball of your thumb against the side of your index finger. Stiffen the thumb and jab it into the opponent's rib cage, rubbing it up and down over the thinly clad bones. Use this same weapon to press against the temples or

Fig. 99 Flick your fingers across the opponent's eyes, so he is forced to turn his head away.

Fig. 100 Thrust down with your left foot and lever him away with your right knee.

sides of the jaw. Break a grip by driving it into the back of the opponent's hand. Keys can also be used to achieve the same result.

If you are on the floor and the opponent is standing over you, then your first consideration is to make safe. Keep your eyes on the opponent and bring your elbows in. Protect your face and head with both forearms and roll onto one hip. Paddle yourself around, so the opponent never has a clear shot at your head, groin or kidneys. Lash out with your heels whenever he gets close, aiming to strike his thighs or groin (fig. 101).

Fig. 101 Each time he gets too close, lash out with your heels. Turn yourself to follow his every movement.

Few adults can defend themselves adequately in a prone position. The Police Self-Defence System therefore includes lessons in tactical thinking whilst an individual is on the ground. Not all the techniques taught have a direct self-defence application, but form a basis for practice which will have a direct skill transference to street fighting.

SPORT TECHNIQUES

Practising the sport techniques of aikido is an excellent way of training for the self-defence situation. Though there is a world of difference between the stylised attacks and defence responses of a combat sport, and the rough and tumble danger of a real-life attack, there are enough similarities to make the exercise worthwhile. In the first instance, sport techniques are unprogrammed insofar as the attacker can choose from a repertoire available to him. Therefore, as defender you are obliged to take each technique as it comes and to make the best of it. The similarities between this and true self-defence are obvious.

Secondly, your opponent in sport-aikido is not going to wait around while you fumble for a hold. If you don't get the response right, then too bad! Although this resembles the street situation, if you get it wrong, you can always try again later. There is an element, therefore, of urgency and realism (but not of finality!) to your responses that programmed sparring simply can't inculcate.

Sport aikido techniques teach students how to deal with an unco-operative opponent. This is the closest one can get to the actual self-defence situation in real life. No amount of prearranged practice can substitute for it.

Five aikido and five judo techniques make up the sport section for the Police Self-Defence System and five have been selected for inclusion in this book. The opponent uses a rubber knife and is able to score a point by striking you in the chest with a straight, lunging action.

In the first sequence, the opponent steps forwards with his right foot and lunges forwards with the rubber knife, aiming to strike you around belt height. Step to the left, but not so far that you can't reach the knife-wielding arm with your left hand. Bar the knife away with the little finger edge of your hand (fig. 102). Strike the opponent in the right shoulder with the flat of your right hand, pushing him backwards and off balance (fig. 103). Keep an eye on the position of that knife at all times! Step strongly forwards, thrust-

Above **Fig. 102** Deflect the knife-wielding arm with the little finger edge of your left hand.

Above, right **Fig. 103** Strike him in the shoulder with your right palm.

Fig. 104 Step forwards and lift the opponent's right knee with your left hand, pushing him backwards and off balance.

ing hard into the opponent's shoulder and tipping him further back. Slide your left hand under his knee and lift even as you push (fig. 104).

This technique, like those which follow, depends for its success upon the speed with which you respond. Move too early and the opponent will simply change his aim. Move too slowly and the knife gets you! Move too far away and you won't be able to close quickly enough to unbalance him. Don't move far enough and the knife will score in you! The technique isn't over when you evade the knife thrust: it terminates only when the opponent is on his back. Therefore, don't take time to congratulate yourself for deflecting the knife. Press on and unbalance him.

The second technique begins from a similar attack and evasion. Note how the right hand is also in a guarding position should the front hand fail to deflect (fig. 105). Spring forwards so your left thigh jams behind the opponent's right, barring his chest with your left arm and controlling the knee with your right (fig. 106). The knife hand is wedged between your left ribs and the opponent's waist. Force your left arm back, so the opponent is tipped diagonally backwards and over your left thigh (fig. 107).

This technique will only work if you close distance after the knife deflection. If the front of your thigh doesn't smack into his leg, then you will be obliged to reach for him and leverage will be lost.

Fig. 105 Note the rear guarding hand. It is there to offer a second line of defence should the leading arm fail to deflect the attack.

Below, left **Fig. 106** Jam behind the opponent's right knee with your left knee, bringing your left arm across his chest.

Below **Fig. 107** Bar the opponent over your left thigh.

The third technique uses the now familiar opening move after which you quickly swivel your hips until you are both facing in the same direction. Keep your left hand on his arm (fig. 108) and slide it down to take his wrist in such a way that the thumb crosses the back of his hand. Swing your left leg quickly around and reinforce your hold on his wrist with your right hand, so the two thumbs cross each other (fig. 109). Continue to swing your left foot around and bend his wrist so the knife point is turned back towards him (fig. 110).

Do not execute this technique too forcefully, because the turning action used can generate a very powerful leverage. Keep your elbows to your sides as you apply the technique, otherwise you will not be able to apply leverage correctly. Avoid twisting the opponent's elbow outwards, because this is

Above **Fig. 108** Step around as you deflect the knife thrust, keeping your hold on the opponent's right wrist.

Above, right **Fig. 109** Step around with your back leg, reinforcing your grip on the opponent's wrist.

Fig. 110 Continue to swing your left foot around and bend the opponent's wrist so the fingers point back to his shoulder.

not as effective as flexing his wrist so that the fingers point back at his shoulder.

The fourth technique used a sidestep evasion to knife thrust, blocking underneath the attacking arm and securing the opponent's wrist with your rear guarding hand (fig. 111). Step up with your back foot, raising the opponent's forearm and reinforcing your grip with the right hand. Rotate the

Fig. 111   Block under the attacking arm with your leading guard hand and take the opponent's wrist with your right hand.

Below, left **Fig. 112**   Step forwards, lifting and twisting the opponent's forearm in a double-handed grip.

Below **Fig. 113**   Continue stepping through and pull the opponent's arm diagonally down and behind him.

trapped wrist so the knife turns inwards and points at the opponent's leading thigh (fig. 112). This exerts a painful leverage, bringing the opponent up and onto his toes. Immediately step through with the left leg and draw the opponent's arm diagonally backwards, so he is taken off balance (fig. 113) and falls to the floor.

The key to this response lies in the phased step forwards that first raises the opponent to a point of precarious balance, and then takes him diagonally backwards. Maintain a strong grip of his wrist with both hands throughout.

The fifth and last of the sport-aikido techniques uses the same opening response as the previous sequence. The knife arm is taken in both hands and the opponent's forearm is raised to bring him onto tip toe (fig. 114). Note, however, that you have not stepped forwards and consequently his elbow is not taken so high. Draw his arm strongly downwards (fig. 115) and release your right grip. Turn your body sharply so that your right side comes against

Fig. 114 Take the opponent's wrist up and back, but do not step towards him.

Fig. 115 The opponent steps back to straighten his arm as you pull it downwards.

his chest as you push your right arm under his (fig. 116). Swivel your hips strongly to your left and bend your knees to drop under his centre of gravity. Pull strongly down and across on his right arm whilst levering up with your right (fig. 117). This will draw him up and over your shoulder to land on his back in front of you.

A set of competition rules employing these and related techniques will be found later in this book.

Fig. 116 Twist your body sharply, driving your right hand under the opponent's upper arm.

Fig. 117 Drop under the opponent's centre of gravity and lever him up and over, using a twisting action of the upper body, a lifting pressure applied with the right arm and a pulling action of the left hand.

THROWING TECHNIQUES

The throwing techniques described in this chapter are taken from the combat sport of judo. They illustrate useful points with regard to balance and leverage. Before practising, check that the training area is large enough and matted to prevent injury. Wherever possible, students should be matched size for size.

> **Judo throwing techniques use leverage and balance to overturn the opponent.**
> The grappling that goes with these throws is a useful concomitant to self-defence training.

No. 1

The first judo throw is known as a leg reap. Take up the opening position with your right hand grasping the opponent's left lapel and your left hand holding his sleeve at about elbow level. The opponent will hold on to you in the same way (fig.118). Change your right hand position, grasping the opponent's collar instead of his sleeve and smoothly draw him towards you (fig.119). Then throw your weight forwards, crashing your right shoulder into his chest. Note that your head should be thrust forwards (fig.120). Step forwards with your right foot and hook backwards into the opponent's right leg, so the back of your knee contacts the back of the opponent's knee (fig.121). Pull on the opponent's right sleeve and twist your right hip into the movement. Push and lift with your right hand at the same time. The result of this will be to unbalance the opponent diagonally backwards. Release the opponent's collar, but retain hold of his sleeve, so he cannot roll away from you.

The inexperienced opponent may keep hold of your lapel in the hope of bringing you down, too. In so doing, his chance to breakfall properly is lost and he may also have the impact of your falling body to contend with. A strong opponent may thrust his weight forwards against you. Stop this from happening by forcing his head back as yours moves forwards.

More advanced students may choose to set the opponent up correctly for the throw by drawing him forwards gently until he steps forwards on his

Fig. 118 Throwing technique no. 1. Your left hand grasps the opponent's right sleeve. The right hand takes his lapel.

Fig. 119 Grasp the opponent's collar and draw him towards you.

Fig. 120 Drive your head forwards and 'crash' your right shoulder into the opponent's chest.

Fig. 121 Hook the opponent's back leg as you push him diagonally backwards over it.

right leg. The step then required to execute the throw is much shortened and the effort required is less than it would be if there were a larger gap between them.

No. 2

The second throw is slightly more complicated than the first. Begin from the ready posture by pulling on the opponent's right sleeve and lifting slightly with your right hand. Slide your left foot to the left and turn the toes outwards, then pivot to your left, bringing your right foot quickly across and in front of the opponent's (fig.122). Swing your leg backwards in a lifting motion as you simultaneously drag on his sleeve and push with your right hand (fig.123). The fulcrum is the upper part of your thigh and, as the opponent has more weight above it than below, he will fall fowards over your leg.

Fig. 122 Throwing technique no. 2. Bring your right foot across and in front of the opponent's.

Fig. 123 Twist and pull him forwards over your right thigh.

No. 3

The third throw begins with a gentle pull on the opponent's tunic to make him stiffen slightly. Then slide your right foot across in front of his (fig.124), releasing your grip on his lapel and thrusting your right arm under his (fig.125). Turn your head and shoulders well to the left until your back smacks into the opponent's stomach (fig.126). Straighten your slightly bent knees to lift him, pulling with your left hand and lifting with your right.

Above **Fig. 124** Throwing technique no. 3. Slide your right foot across and in front of the opponent's

Above, right **Fig. 125** Thrust your right hand under the opponent's upper arm.

Fig. 126 Drop under the opponent's centre of gravity, then straighten your knees, lifting him up and over.

More skilled students will draw the opponent forwards, so that he steps with his left leg. Begin turning even as the opponent moves, which means that as the step is completed, your back is full against him. Bringing your right elbow up hard under his arm will take the opponent to the tips of his toes and make him stoop forwards, ready for the throw.

No. 4

The fourth throw uses a strong pull with your left hand to draw the opponent forwards. Slide your right hand into a collar grip and begin twisting your body in an anti-clockwise direction (fig.127). Thrust your right foot forwards so that it comes past the opponent's right ankle and twist your body further, dragging him over his front leg (fig.128). The opponent virtually rolls over your right thigh and falls onto his back in front of you.

You must turn your hips in such a way that your left foot faces in the same direction as the opponent. Your hips must drop under the opponent's stomach and there must be a straight line between your right ankle, knee, hip and shoulder. Your right leg is used as an obstacle over which the opponent is made to tumble, so bring your right calf as low as possible under the opponent's knee. Then when your leg straightens, the opponent's foot is lifted from the mat; since this is the leg he is standing on, you will soon gain the advantage!

Fig. 127 Throwing technique no. 4. Slide your right hand into a collar grip and draw the opponent across your front by pulling with your left hand.

Fig. 128 Drag the opponent over his own front leg, using the back of your right thigh as the fulcrum.

No. 5

The final throw is an extremely powerful technique that invariably finishes with both partners on the floor. Begin from the ready posture, securing the back of the opponent's collar. Twist your hips strongly to your left and bring your left foot into the centre line in front of and between the opponent's (fig. 129). Turn sharply so that your back is presented to the opponent. Pull strongly across with your left hand and push up with the right. As you do this, thrust your stiffened right leg high between his thighs (fig. 130). This will jar him into the air and allow you to pull him forwards and off-balance.

Fig. 129   Throwing technique no. 5. Twist your hips strongly and put your right foot in front of and between the opponent's feet.

Fig. 130   Continue the hip action so your right thigh slams back into the opponent's upper leg, jarring him from the ground.

THE NATURE OF
SELF-DEFENCE

'Self-defence' means different things to different people. The purpose of this section is to identify briefly what does and does not constitute 'self-defence'. As a working definition, the term 'self-defence' can be applied to any system of techniques designed, in the first instance, to avoid and, in the second instance, to respond effectively to actual or implied violence against oneself. Without doubt, the best form of self-defence lies in recognising and avoiding hazard. However, it is not always possible to do this; in which case, practical techniques may have some value.

Sometimes the term 'unarmed combat' is encountered. As its name implies, unarmed combat is a fighting system which makes use of the body's weapons. Unarmed combat teaches both how to attack and how to defend. There are various forms of unarmed combat, most of which are taught in the Armed Forces. Clearly some unarmed combat techniques could be used or adapted for self-defence purposes. However, since self-defence may well involve the usage of weapons, unarmed combat would clearly not be able to provide experience in this area.

The term 'martial art' is often associated with self-defence. In normal usage, it describes fighting systems that originated in the Far East, but this is not the exact definition. In fact, a 'martial art' is any codified set of techniques which are, or have been, used by the military. The latter description, however, eliminates many of what are nowadays taken to be 'martial arts'. Be all that as it may, the general application of the term includes a mixture of religio-philosophic systems and combat sports, none of which can be said to have an immediate application to modern day self-defence. This is not, however, to say that certain of their techniques could not be so applied.

If is an unfortunate fact that in any situation of actual physical encounter, the more aggressive, stronger and fitter participant will stand a better chance of prevailing. One must accept that though skill in applying self-defence techniques may go some way towards redressing the imbalance, there is no guarantee that it will sway the outcome decisively in the victim's favour.

Having said that, there is no doubt that an aggressively applied self-defence technique will work in certain circumstances; but one should not be over-confident. Unfortunately, the only way of knowing just how effective that technique will be is by applying it during a genuine attack. At least the techniques included in this book have a foundation insofar as they have been tested by a variety of people in a wide area of actual attack circumstances. No other self-defence system presently available to the general public can claim a similar foundation. The longer the course, the more effective the techniques used and the greater the students' application, then the greater will be the potential benefit.

Despite this, it is worth reiterating that mastery of physical techniques will not *ipso facto* make the student into an effective exponent of self-defence.

EVALUATING A SELF-DEFENCE SYSTEM

The purpose of this section is to provide a self-help guide for people wishing to take up self-defence. Nowadays, self-defence courses are being offered by a wide variety of organisations and one means of threading a way through the conflicting claims which each makes is to look at the core principles involved.

Finding a place to practise self-defence

Are the premises suitable for practice? They should be warm, dry, well-ventilated and, above all, not overcrowded. The floor area should be free of hazards and mats should be provided for safe landings. Practice should be friendly but disciplined. The coach must be properly qualified to teach self-defence; he should hold an appropriate registration with Taiho jutsu, a self-defence coaching qualification from the Martial Arts Commission, or a similar endorsement from the British Judo Association.

In the long term, it probably is the case that practice of a martial art *will* lead to an improved self-defence capability, but that capability is conferred only after many years. In fact, practice of a martial art is neither a necessary nor a sufficient foundation for an effective self-defence system.

Some people feel happier with a male coach; others, with a female. Ultimately, choice will be dictated by availability. However, if one accepts the axiom that a self-defence course must strive, wherever possible, for realism, then a female would-be participant should always seek mixed classes. For a woman, the experience of training with a male partner is closer to reality than training with another female.

Courses

In general terms, the shorter a self-defence course, the less ground can be covered. It is not feasible to give an optimum length for a course, since one that sets out to teach five techniques to an adequate skill level will take less time than another which aims at teaching twenty-five. Provided those twenty-five techniques are carefully selected, then it follows that the larger course will have a wider application. If the participant has only a limited time, then the shorter course with only a few techniques will prove more useful.

Some techniques are harder to execute than others. This, however, is not a problem, since no one is expected to perform all the techniques to exactly the same skill level. The target to aim for is good proficiency in just three or four techniques.

Skill is obtained through repetition of an action. The more times that action is repeated, the more likely it is to be performed correctly. Rest periods play an important role, because skills are most quickly taken up by a rested neuro-muscular system. It therefore follows that the best courses to enrol on are those with frequent, short lessons. Concentrated courses are less effective for the majority of people. Sometimes a training block is encountered and progress comes to a halt. Sidestep the block by going on to practise other techniques.

Observing and assessing

Without doubt, the first line of self-defence is observation and assessment. Observation is used here in the sense of simply being aware of the surroundings. Although this sounds self-evident, it is surprising how preoccupied people can be. Observation is something which may need to be cultivated until it becomes a habit. At first it requires conscious effort, but later it becomes a part of life.

Assessment is the way in which information obtained through observation is processed. By means of this procedure, extraneous stimuli are filtered out and relevant ones are retained. The latter provide the basis for an assessment of whether an approaching situation is hazard-free, potentially hazardous, or actually hazardous. All good self-defence courses must include at least one workshop or seminar on these two important aspects of self-defence.

Mental attitude

Having the correct mental attitude is also important. It is one thing to possess the skill to repulse an attack; it is quite another to be mentally able to use that skill. A comprehensive self-defence course will therefore deal with the psychology of assertion. Poor self-defence courses build a false confidence which is founded upon satisfactory performance of techniques in a convivial atmosphere. This can be dangerous insofar as it may lead to faulty evaluation of one's own capabilities.

Systems

A good self-defence course must operate according to a logical and flexible system. Whatever the attack, it should be dealt with in such a way as to bring it into a familiar response pattern. Moreover, a fail-safe must always be incorporated so that if a response fails, the participant is left in a position of relative personal safety and with a potential follow-up technique as additional back-up. By comparison, the poor course is no more than a general collection of techniques, each requiring its own particular application.

The techniques employed by a self-defence system must be relevant. It would be difficult for a non-pilot to write an authoritative book on the practical aspects of flying. Yet few authors of self-defence systems can claim a sufficient breadth of experience on which to found their systems. A 95 kg (209½ lb) weightlifter may have been picked on sufficient times to allow him to work out a valid self-defence system, but what evidence does he have that his system will work equally well for a 45 kg (99 lb) female?

Checklist for evaluating a self-defence course

The following is a ten-point checklist to enable you to decide whether a local self-defence course is worth attending.

1 Is the training venue suitable for the purpose? Is it overcrowded? Are training mats provided?
2 Is the coach properly qualified to teach self-defence? Is he a registered coach with the Martial Arts Commission?
3 Is an insurance indemnity included within your course fee?
4 Do you have the time to complete the course?
5 Is the course able to accommodate the odd absence from a lesson?
6 Is training intensity within your capabilities? This is to say, will you be spending all of your time trying to keep up with the class, leaving none to acquire the skill you are seeking?
7 Does the course include workshops on observation/assessment and on assertion (or a related form of mental training)?

8 Does the course operate to a system? Are unfamiliar attacks dealt with by a relatively small number of responses, or is each species of attack met with a highly specific response?
9 Are the attacks realistic? For example, is it likely that a strangle from the rear would be applied with straight arms?
10 Are the responses, as taught, within your physical capabilities?

THE MARTIAL ARTS COMMISSION

It is possible for any person to set up a self-defence course, whether he has knowledge or not. Interestingly, so far no one has been prosecuted for falsely misrepresenting himself as a proficient coach, though it would be theoretically possible to bring such an action. Many self-defence courses currently being offered are of dubious standard and it is regrettable that some local authorities and education authorities have been persuaded to sponsor them.

The majority of these courses are poor in the sense that they contain few elements of value. Some are poor insofar as they charge a lot of money for very little instruction. A minority are dangerous and, in one or two reported cases, students have been physically and sexually abused.

Since the single most important step a student will take is to select a good course, it follows that expert advice is essential. Such advice is available from the Martial Arts Commission, Broadway House, 15–16 Deptford Broadway, London SE8 4PE (tel: 01 691 3433). The Commission was set up in 1977 and one of its objectives is to regulate and control the practice of martial arts (and self-defence) in the United Kingdom. The Commission has devised its own self-defence system, based on the programme given in this book. Self-defence coaches are properly qualified and the course operates at a fixed cost which includes per capita insurance. Write to the Commission, enclosing a stamped addressed envelope, and you will be sent details of your nearest course.

Alternatively, contact the British Taiho Jutsu Association, via the Martial Arts Commission. The Association independently qualifies and registers self-defence coaches in the police system described in the book. A further alternative is the British Judo Association, whose address is 16 Upper Woburn Place, London SW1. The B.J.A. has set up its own course to a national syllabus and this is worth considering.

TRAINING SAFETY

Fitness

Self-defence courses involve a sustained level of physical activity which you must be fit enough to maintain for the whole of the lesson. If your everyday job is physically demanding, then the requirements of training will not be excessive. If, however, you lead a sedentary lifestyle, then those same requirements may prove onerous. Skill acquisition is best achieved when the body is not tired, so it follows that if you are not fit enough to cope, it may be a good idea to delay enrolling until you are.

You can become sufficiently fit by means of a light programme of jogging, swimming, or cycling; but whichever you choose, be prepared to spend twenty minutes each day doing it. Regulate your pace so you can last the full twenty minutes, and, as fitness improves, so the amount of work you are able to manage will increase.

Health

The above paragraphs presuppose that you are healthy. If you are not healthy, or have not had a check-up for some time, then it may be a good idea to visit the doctor prior to commencement of training. He will be in a position to advise you whether to enrol or not. Declare any health conditions beforehand to the self-defence coach, since this will allow him to monitor your performance. The following health conditions *must* be notified:

- heart problems
- asthma
- diabetes
- epilepsy.

Do not train if you suffer from haemophilia or related blood-clotting disorders. The techniques of self-defence may cause bleeding into the joint capsules and other more serious complications. If you are taking any medication, then carry a supply into the training hall. This applies especially to asthma sufferers. Diabetics should bring some lemonade or their usual glucose supply. Grand mal epileptics should train only when the floor is padded.

Influenza and colds are good reasons for temporarily stopping training. This is because some types of virus make the heart muscle excitable and prone to irregularity. One known fatality has resulted from a martial arts student receiving a hard bang in the chest whilst suffering from 'flu. Cover all cuts and abrasions with a suitable dressing.

Do not train if at any time in the last six weeks you have suffered from a head injury which knocked you senseless. Such an injury will have destroyed brain cells and a period of rest is necessary for others to take over the dead cells' functions. If this rest is not granted and the head is subjected to further injury, the damage will be compounded and will take much longer to heal.

Clothing

Wear suitable loose, everyday clothes for training, but ensure these are strong enough to withstand the to-ing and fro-ing they will receive. Track suits or judo tunics are ideal. Whatever you choose, make sure it has no buckles or any other sharp objects which might cause injury. You will not be able to wear shoes if mats are in use, but in case they are not, light trainers are the most suitable footwear.

Remove watches, earrings and other jewellery before training begins. Tape over rings which you cannot take off. Empty your pockets of sharp metallic objects. Secure long hair with an elastic band and *not* with a metal fastener. Keep finger- and toe-nails short, and be assiduous about your hygiene. Spectacles must be removed, though they can be slipped on during technique demonstrations. Contact lenses can be worn, but they seldom stay in place.

Practice

Start and stop training promptly on command, and only practise the techniques which you have been shown. Look after your partner and work at a speed that both of you can comfortably manage. Such speed ought to allow you to perform techniques correctly. Don't worry about working at high speed – that comes later.

If you are larger than your partner, take care to avoid causing unwitting injury through the sheer power of your techniques. Be especially careful when throwing a partner. Remember: the object is always to control your partner, not to inflict injury! Immediately cease applying a technique when your partner submits. Submission is indicated by tapping a partner or a mat.

Aim all attacks at the target and do not be tempted to help your partner by aiming slightly to the side. All the latter will do is to teach your partner how to respond to an off-centre attack. Increase training intensity and your standard will increase correspondingly.

Notify the coach if you suffer any injury during training and refrain from further training if it is likely to make the injury worse.

STRIKING AND GRAPPLING TECHNIQUES

Striking techniques play only a minor role in the Police Self-Defence System. One of the reasons for this is that there is something not entirely acceptable about a police officer punching and kicking a member of the public. Another reason is that striking techniques do not give the kind of controlled response to aggression that the Service requires. Therefore, when striking techniques are used, they tend to be secondary and of a distracting nature. However, having said that, the system does include two kicking techniques and a knee attack, all of which could do more than distract.

Another problem with striking techniques is that while people can quickly learn how to deliver a powerful blow, the body weapons themselves are likely to suffer injury. What is the use of being able to strike with a lot of force if every time you do so your wrist or knuckles fracture? High power hand techniques must be accurately targeted, otherwise the wrong part of your fist will make contact with the wrong part of the opponent.

Kicking techniques are certainly less susceptible to injury as long as you use the padded parts of your foot. But how safe are you when standing on one leg? Clearly you should use kicks only when you are outside punching range.

The Police Self-Defence System relies upon grappling techniques as its mainstay. This is because, on purely social grounds, they can be controlled more effectively than striking techniques and the chance of injury is reduced. Secondly, they allow the opponent to be restrained rather than injured. Thirdly, the kind of distances that real-life self-defence encounters take place over tend not to favour striking techniques.

However, grappling techniques suffer one major disadvantage over striking techniques: they require a higher skill level to perform effectively. Without wishing to disparage strike-based self-defence systems, their techniques are much simpler, albeit more restricted in application.

Grappling techniques use the principles of leverage, so a minimum of applied force produces the maximum of effect. To capitalise on this means applying force as far from the fulcrum as possible. Therefore, when applying a gooseneck hold to your partner's wrist, first try applying pressure near his wrist joint. Then apply the same pressure, but close to his knuckles. In the second instance you will have moved away from the fulcrum (the wrist joint) and leverage is increased.

A second consideration is the nature of the joint which you are attacking. A strong opponent might be able to 'unwind' an arm entangle hold applied by a much weaker person. This is simply because the arm joints attacked by this hold are all well muscled. However, even the weakest person can hold a powerful opponent by attacking the thumb joint – provided, of course, that you can secure a firm enough grip of it! The wrist, too, is comparatively weak and vulnerable to attack. It is also at the end of the arm and so is easier to take hold of and apply leverage to.

TAIHO JUTSU
COMPETITION RULES

In order to test self-defence techniques, it is necessary to find an opponent who is going to behave in an unexpected yet relatively safe way. Free sparring and competition provide an approximation to the self-defence situation and so they are an important part of the training syllabus. However, there is still a wide gulf between the rule-governed operation of free sparring and the totally free self-defence situation. Unfortunately, there is simply no other way to test safely the techniques. Therefore, these rules have been instituted to allow students of Taiho jutsu to test their skills in a safe and enjoyable way.

The first requirement of the competition is that it must take place on a matted square, nine metres along each side. A further metre wide surrounding strip of mats will serve as a safety area. The mats used must be capable of safely absorbing the impact of a falling body and they must fit together for all of their length, so that no gaps capable of trapping ankles can open up. The competition area must be level and free of hazard.

Contestants must wear clean white or cream uniforms of a type approved by the tournament organiser. These uniforms must be in a good stage of repair, otherwise a contestant may be disbarred from the competition. Female contestants may wear a clean white and unfigured teeshirt beneath the jacket. One contestant should wear a red belt and the other, a white belt. Contestants must keep their nails short and they may not wear any object which might, in the opinion of the referee, pose a threat of injury. Such prohibited articles include jewellery, such as rings, bracelets and metal hair clips. Long hair must be secured with an elastic band. Spectacles are prohibited, but contestants may wear soft contact lenses on their own responsibility.

Each match will be supervised from within the area by a referee appointed by the tournament organiser. Two judges will be positioned outside the area, on the corners near the officials' side of the mat. Each judge will have a red and a white flag. The time of each match will be kept by a timekeeper and he will sound an audible warning at 'time up'. The match will be of four one-minute rounds, but in the event of a tied score, an extension of two further one-minute rounds may be fought. Time is automatically stopped whenever there is an interruption.

One contestant has a rubber knife of a type authorised by the tournament organiser. This contestant is referred to as *tanto*. The unarmed contestant is referred to as *toshu*. The first *tanto* of any match will be the contestant wearing the red belt. The knife is collected from the referee at the commencement of each round and is returned to him at the end of the match. The contestants stand four metres apart, red on the referee's right, white on his left. The match opens with an exchange of bows between the officials and the contestants, after which the latter turn to face each other and perform a second bow. This procedure is reversed at the end of the match.

Points are scored when *toshu* applies a standing technique, or when *tanto* scores with a legitimate knife thrust. A majority agreement of the officials witnessing the technique is necessary to award a score. In the case of a tied opinion, the referee's will prevail. Five points are awarded if *toshu* correctly performs a technique or a recognised variation of the Taiho jutsu syllabus. Five points may also be awarded if *tanto* submits. Three points will be awarded if the technique is slightly deficient in some aspect of its execution, or when *toshu* scores with a sacrifice throw. Three points will also be awarded if *toshu* breaks the opponent's balance and gains control through a restraining technique, but *tanto* is not taken to the mat. Three points will be awarded if both contestants fall to the mat and one succeeds in holding the other in a groundwork technique for twenty seconds, or if a submission is gained through a straight- or bent-lock to either arm or leg.

Tanto will score one point for a correct knife strike to *toshu's* scoring area. This area is defined as being from the top of the shoulders to the waist, and covering both the back and chest/stomach. The knife thrust must be made from *tanto's* centre hip line and it must touch the target area with the arm extended and the knife horizontal. *Tanto's* hips and shoulders must be square behind the thrust and both feet must travel forwards behind it. *Tanto* must push his hips forwards behind the strike. If *toshu* covers the target area with a hand and fails to use a proper deflection technique, then a score will be awarded, even if the knife strikes the masking limb(s). *Toshu's* response to a knife thrust is limited to avoidance and/or deflecting *tanto's* forearm with a forearm block. No score will be awarded if *toshu* merely deflects the strike.

The first contestant to amass ten points will be declared the winner; if neither does, then the contestant with the most points will receive the decision. If the scores are equal at the end of the match, the extension rounds will be fought and scores obtained will be added to those already held in order to find a winner. If scores remain tied, despite this, the referee will consult with the judges and a majority decision will be given in favour of one contestant. The basis for this superiority will include such factors as better fighting spirit, more vigorous attacks and more evidence of skill.

Points may only be scored during match time. If time expires but the referee fails to notice, then the match may continue but no scores will be awarded. If a score is made at the same time that time up is called, the score will be recorded. During the course of a technique, the contestant scored upon may leave the area, but this shall not nullify the score provided that the scorer remained within the boundary. If both *tanto* and *toshu* simultaneously score upon each other, no score will be awarded.

If either contestant goes to the mat following an accident or an attempted technique, both may attempt to score by a hold down. The time limit for groundwork is fifteen seconds, after which the match is interrupted and both contestants are returned to a standing position. If a hold is applied during the fifteen seconds, its progress will be monitored by the referee for the twenty-second period, or until the hold is broken. The rules of judo competition will be applied to groundwork, except that strangles are not permitted whereas leg locks are. However, no leg lock may be applied which puts lateral strain on the joint.

If either or both contestants perform a prohibited act, the referee will stop the match and give a warning or impose a penalty or a disqualification. Two penalties may be awarded, the first meriting a one point deduction and the second, a three point deduction. A further infringement will merit automatic disqualification from that match. This doesn't preclude the referee from immediately imposing a disqualification for serious infringements.

Contestants may not punch or kick each other and neither should they use any technique considered by the referee to be dangerous. Examples of this might be performing a sacrifice throw whilst applying a joint-locking technique, deliberately falling onto an opponent, or applying a stranglehold. Only techniques from the Taiho jutsu syllabus are allowed; all others will attract a penalty. Neither contestant may engage in timewasting behaviour, such as when *tanto* does not persistently attack, or uses the knife incorrectly, or when *toshu* continually shortens distance, which prevents *tanto* from making a scoring strike.

Neither contestant may attempt to evade a technique by stepping out of the match area; nor should one contestant try to push the other out. *Tanto* is restricted to using the knife in the approved manner and he may not try to counter *toshu*'s attacks, except when both are in the groundwork position. All *toshu*'s techniques must avoid gripping *tanto*'s tunic during their execution.

Contestants must always behave with respect towards each other and the referee is empowered to take the severest action if this behaviour lapses.

It is not possible to protest about the outcome of a match, though an official representative of a contestant may query the application of the rules on any point. This should be done after the match in which the protest has been generated and the two contestants involved should not proceed any further through the draw until the matter has been resolved. The contestant's representative must make the protest to an arbitrator appointed by the tournament organiser and, if it is felt appropriate, he will call the referee for an explanation. The team representative should be disbarred from the discussion between the arbitrator and the referee, but should be immediately notified of the outcome. The arbitrator and referee have the power to reverse a decision in a protested match, or to take such action as may be necessary to redress error. In the event of a disagreement between the arbitrator and referee, the latter's decision is final.

In case of administrative or scoring errors, the contestant's representative may directly approach the scorekeeper's table. Such errors are when points have been wrongly totalled, or when the wrong contestant is called to the mat.

In the event of injury, the referee will stop the match and will examine the contestant to see whether first aid is necessary. Should the referee fail to note an injury, the judges may attract his attention. If first aid is required, a doctor will be summoned and he will afterwards advise the referee concerning the injury. The referee has the power to withdraw an injured contestant if he considers that to fight on will exacerbate the injury. Feigning injury is a serious offence against the match rules.

If the injury is the fault of an opponent, then he will be appropriately penalised. If the injury is not the fault of the opponent but the match cannot continue, the withdrawing contestant will forfeit the match. If both contestants are injured through their own faults and must be withdrawn, then the match will be given to the contestant with the higher score at that point. The tournament doctor is required to authorise all bandages used during the tournament.

The contestants and referee will resume their standing positions when points are to be awarded, when penalties are to be imposed, or when the outcome of a match is to be announced.

THE TAIHO JUTSU GRADING SYLLABUS

One of the most effective ways to maintain interest in training is to use what is known as a 'grading system'. This is a ladder of progression, taking a student from a novice level of skill to a stage of high proficiency. Provided that the requirements between each successive 'rung' of the ladder are not onerous, the student will be able to see for himself that he is making progress.

There is no set time limit between successive gradings; that will depend upon the number of lessons attended each week and the duration of each lesson. Minimum age for entering the grading structure is 16, though parental consent at this age is required.

The Taiho jutsu grading syllabus comprises five coloured belt stages, or **kyu** grades, followed by the black belt. Note that the first and second kyus are each divided into upper and lower levels. There is provision within the syllabus for advancement within the black belt to a fifth level, or **dan**, of ability.

The kyu grades cover the twenty basic techniques, plus five aikido and five judo techniques from the sport side of the syllabus. Requirement for dan grade includes a good level of ability in the kyu grade syllabus plus skill in free play. The higher dan grades require a knowledge of competition, coaching and another martial discipline. This is because the Police Self-Defence System has been derived from various sources and comprises striking techniques, elements of aikido, judo and sombo wrestling.

APPENDIX

KYU GRADES (minimum age, 16 years)

5th Kyu	*Yellow belt*	8 techniques (student's choice) 4 groundwork techniques Basic free play
4th Kyu	*Orange belt*	8 techniques (examiner's choice) 4 left side techniques sparring, one against one
3rd Kyu	*Green belt*	16 techniques complete variations of attack as required sparring, one versus two

2nd Kyu	*Blue belt*	(lower) aikido tanto (5) variations and combinations (upper) free play
1st Kyu	*Brown belt*	(lower) judo techniques (5) variations and combinations (upper) free play

DAN GRADES (minimum age, 18 years)

1st Dan		1st kyu for one year complete knowledge of kyu grade syllabus variations of technique as required
2nd Dan		1st dan for 2 years competition record traditional aikido techniques (20)
3rd Dan		2nd dan for 2 years coaching award koryu no kata (16)
4th Dan		3rd dan for 2 years senior coaching award koryu no kata (34)
5th Dan		4th dan for 2 years dan grade in another discipline koryu no kata (50)

At each grade level, a demonstration of the previous syllabus is required.

INDEX